Flute and Piano

THE WORLD'S GREAT CLASSICAL MUSIC

The Baroque and Classical Flute

12 Favorite Pieces by the Masters

EDITED BY ELAINE SCHMIDT
Bryan Stanley, assistant editor

Cover Painting: Gerrit Adriaensz Berckheyde, *The Castle of Heemstede*, 1662

ISBN 978-0-634-02231-9

HAL•LEONARD®
CORPORATION

7777 W. BLUEMOUND RD. P.O. BOX 13819 MILWAUKEE, WI 53213

Visit Hal Leonard Online at
www.halleonard.com

FOREWORD

Playing Baroque music presents both students and professionals with some interesting challenges. Many composers of the Baroque and Classical eras did not write many, if any, dynamic markings or articulation markings in their music. Nor did they indicate all of the trills or other ornaments that were in common use at the time. If an edition of a Bach piece does not include any of these familiar marks, do not assume the composer wanted the music to be played without dynamic contrasts or expressive articulations. Bach, and other composers of his time, left those details up to the performer. The flutist can make a personal statement in part by deciding how to tongue and slur a piece, or how to use dynamic contrasts.

If you are confused about working out interpretive details for a piece of music, you are not alone. There are no absolute rules, but there are lots of opinions. Two hundred-fifty years ago, musical customs differed from one European country to another, and even from one local province to another. Although many composers used the same symbols for ornaments in their music, the symbols did not necessarily mean the same thing to each composer. Since the technology for recording sound was still hundreds of years away, the musicians who played this music when it was new are silent to us. We will never know exactly how they interpreted the music.

There has been an explosion of interest in early music in recent years, sending scholars and musicians off in search of definitive answers on these topics. The research is like musical detective work. There are written sources such as books and teaching materials from the era to be studied. Original music, preserved in libraries, museums, and other collections, can also provide clues. But for a student today, the best way to learn to play Baroque music, or music of any previous era for that matter, is the same way people learned to play it during the years in which it was new—listening. If you want to play Bach, listen to Bach and if you want to play Handel, listen to Handel. Pay close attention to the details and nuances in the performances and try bringing those ideas to your own playing. Listen to other pieces by the same composer, as well as other composers' pieces written at the same time and in the same country or region. This kind of listening helps create a framework for the musical fashion of the era and the interpretive practices in place today. Understanding how the composer's music fits into the time and place in which it was written is also helpful. Besides traditional library research, the Internet is a great place to search for biographies and histories of musicians and the times in which they lived.

This book provides conservative articulation and dynamic suggestions for the various Baroque and Classical pieces, as well as cadenzas for some of them, to give the student a starting point. As you learn the pieces, you and your teacher may choose to alter these marks and make your own decisions. Feel free. This is part of the fun of playing this music.

—Elaine Schmidt

CONTENTS

* For solo flute, see flute part

CARL PHILIPP EMANUEL BACH (1714-1788)
Sonata in A Minor
> Poco adagio
> Allegro
> Allegro

The second son of Johann Sebastian Bach, C.P.E. Bach is best remembered for his keyboard works and for his treatise, *Versuch über die wahre Art das Clavier spielen* (Essay on the True Art of Playing Keyboard Instruments). The treatise remains a valuable reference on interpretation to this day. He spent twenty-eight years in the service of King Frederick the Great of Prussia, who was an accomplished flutist and composer as well as an avid supporter of the arts. Emanuel was often required to accompany the king's own performances, experiencing tremendous frustration over the restrictions placed upon the music he was required to write for the court.

When he received the king's long-awaited permission to leave the court in 1767, he took a post as music director of the five main churches in Hamburg. Here he found tremendous musical freedom. He developed in much of his music, this unaccompanied sonata included, impulsive melodic and harmonic twists representative of "empfindsamer Stil," the expressive style of composition in the Classical era. Bach once wrote that the human voice was his model for any kind of melodic writing, which can be heard quite clearly in the adagio movement of this piece. In this edition, like the original 1763 publications of this sonata, the adagio movement appears first. In some other editions, this movement is sandwiched by the faster movements.

JOHANN SEBASTIAN BACH (1685-1750)
Partita in A minor, BWV 1013
> Sarabande
> Bourrée Anglaise

Sonata No. 2 in E-flat Major, BWV 1031
> Allegro Moderato
> Siciliano
> Allegro

Suite in B Minor, BWV 1067, selected movements
> Rondeau
> Polonaise
> Menuet
> Badinerie

Johann Sebastian Bach is the name by which many define the late Baroque period. He wrote astounding amounts of church music in addition to orchestral suites, concertos, sonatas and chamber music. Of the pieces included here, the Suite in B Minor and the Partita in A Minor date from his six-year stint as Kapellmeister at the Court of Cöthen, 1717-1723. There were no church music duties for Bach at the court, so he concentrated his efforts on instrumental music. During this time he wrote his Brandenburg Concertos, the four Orchestral Suites and quite a few instrumental sonatas.

Bach is credited with eight flute sonatas, all of which were written for the transverse, or cross-blown, flute as opposed to the recorder that was still popular at the time. The transverse flute was considered a more virtuoso instrument, possibly in part because it could be more easily heard above the sound of a harpsichord or orchestra. The transverse flute also offered the player a broader palette of tonal colors than the recorder. Although there is some question about the authenticity of two of the sonatas, the Sonata No. 2 in E-flat is unquestionably the work of Bach. The sonata better resembles in form the Baroque concerto rather than the Classical sonata later cultivated.

The Suite in B Minor is a work originally for solo flute, orchestra, and continuo written in a style popular with German composers in the early eighteenth century. The musical form has its roots in the French suite, consisting of a grand overture followed by courtly dance movements. Bach's suite opens with a free, slow overture, followed by a series of seven contrasting dance movements, each of which has the unique character of dance forms popular in Bach's time. Bach was one of the first composers to treat the flute seriously. The final movement of the suite, the Badinerie, is some of his most brilliant writing for the instrument.

The lovely Partita in A Minor for unaccompanied flute is something of a mystery. It was discovered during the twentieth century, written in Bach's handwriting on the last page of the manuscript of the six violin solo sonatas. Some scholars are certain that Bach wrote the piece. Others think that it might have been the work of one of his older sons, written while they were studying music with their father. Whichever is the case, it is interesting that C.P.E. Bach later wrote his own unaccompanied flute piece in the same key. The piece is constructed of four dance movements. The sarabande is a highly expressive, lyrical movement that gracefully rolls harmony and melody into a single line. It is followed by a skipping bourrée anglaise.

GEORGE FRIDERIC HANDEL (1685-1759)
Sonata No. 8 in F Major
> Larghetto
> Allegro
> Siciliana
> Allegro

Despite his German background, George Frideric Handel spent the greater part of his life living in England as a composer of opera and English oratorio, his most famous oratorio being *Messiah*. Handel had also spent several years in Italy during his twenties where several of his dramatic works were presented. In 1711 he visited London for the first time, moving there in 1712. Remembered today as one of the greatest composers of his time, he is buried in Westminster Abbey in London.

The flute, actually the "flûte à bec" or recorder, was one of the most popular instruments of the era with both professional and amateur players. A wealth of flute methods was available for purchase, and numerous European composers wrote pieces for the little instrument. Handel too wrote pieces for the flute, including this sonata. The history of his flute sonatas, however, is somewhat confusing. For many years there have been various editions of the "complete" sonatas available, some containing nearly twice as many sonatas as others. To add to the confusion, some sonatas that Handel composed were intended for violin or recorder, and some of his individual movements were reused in other flute sonatas. His sonatas combine Italian, French and German styles and feature keyboard parts that served his own technical expertise as harpsichordist and organist.

FRANZ JOSEPH HAYDN (1732-1809)
Serenade in C Major

Haydn was a pillar of the Austrian musical community and a towering figure in the Classical era. He is remembered as the father of the modern symphony, and was known affectionately by fellow musicians in his day as "Papa."

Widely known as "The Haydn Serenade," this lilting piece first appeared as the "Andante cantabile" movement of his string quartet, Op. 3, No 5. Today it is performed by orchestras as well as by various solo instruments with piano. However, it seems likely that Haydn did not actually write it. It is now believed to be more plausible that a Benedictine monk named Roman Hoffstetter wrote several of the Op. 3 quartets, including No. 5. Hoffstetter, also a composer of string quartets, orchestral and sacred music, is known to have praised Haydn in his writings and to have modeled his quartets after those of the master.

WOLFGANG AMADEUS MOZART (1756-1791)
Andante in C Major, K 315(285e)

Concerto No. 1 in G Major, K 313(285c)
>   First Movement

Concerto No. 2 in D Major, K 314(285d)
>   Second Movement
>   Third Movement

The great Mozart was not fond of the flute. To understand this aversion one must realize that during his lifetime the flute was going through something of an awkward adolescence. The Baroque flute was too limited for the classical orchestra. Flute makers were fashioning flutes out of everything from wood and various metals, to ceramic and glass. Even the number of keys found on the instrument was in flux. When an orchestra hired a flutist, there was no telling what sort of instrument might arrive. The money offered by a commission from a Dutch amateur flutist named Ferdinand de Jean made Mozart put aside his feelings and write these two concertos for flute and orchestra. It is believed that Mozart wrote the Andante in C to replace the Adagio movement from the G Major concerto, which de Jean disliked. The D Major Concerto is likely a transcription of a concerto in C for oboe, although that score has been lost. Mozart uses the rondo-allegro theme in Blondchen's aria "Welche Wonne, welche Lust" in his opera *Die Entführung aus dem Serail* (Abduction from the Seraglio).

JOHANN JOACHIM QUANTZ (1697-1773)
Sonata No. 1 in A Minor
>   Adagio
>   Presto
>   Gigue (Allegro)

Although the German composer Johann Joachim Quantz began his professional life as an oboist, playing in the Polish chapel of Augustus III, he soon turned to the transverse flute. He became a member of the Dresden Court Kapelle as a flutist, soon traveling to Berlin to give flute lessons to Prince Frederick, who would later become King Frederick the Great of Prussia. In 1740 Frederick, then king, employed Quantz to make flutes for him and to write music and oversee concerts. Although Quantz wrote more than 300 concertos, more than 200 sonatas and approximately 60 trio sonatas, all for the flute, he is perhaps most famous for his treatise, *Versuch einer Answeisung die Flöte traversiere zu spielen* (On Playing the Flute). In this work he gives detailed instructions on flute playing and on the execution of ornamental figures common in music of the time. The work has become an indispensable reference for all instrumentalists and is still in print today.

GEORG PHILIPP TELEMANN (1681-1767)

Fantasie No. 2 in A Minor (from 12 Fantasies)
Suite in A minor
      Overture
      Menuet 2

German composer Georg Philipp Telemann was more popular during his lifetime than his illustrious contemporaries Bach and Handel. Although he composed his first opera at age twelve, his interests were not only musical. He studied modern languages, geometry, and law. Later he founded the first German language music journal. By the time of his death, at age 86, he had written more music than any other major composer to date, and had written in every form available to him, from opera and oratorio to chamber music, marches, and ceremonial music. His musical style conformed to the evolving artistic trends of his time, spanning from the Baroque to the Rococo styles, and eventually to the Classical style as modeled by Haydn and C.P.E. Bach.

The Suite in A Minor was likely written in 1737, after Telemann had visited Paris. Like Bach's Suite in B Minor, the piece features an Overture followed by several dance movements. Telemann chose colorful titles for some movements, such as Les Plaisirs (pleasures, delights, or entertainments) and Réjouissance (rejoicing or merry-making), rather than giving the pieces functional titles.

Composed in 1732 and 1733, the twelve fantasies for solo flute are as eclectic as anything the composer ever wrote. In the confines of this collection of perfect miniatures, he incorporated Italian, French, and German styles, moving between the musical conventions of the Baroque and Rococo eras. Within the short movements, some of which are just a few measures long, he balances elegant melody with interesting harmonic motion and color. These pieces, long a favorite of flutists, have been borrowed and transcribed for several other instruments.

Sonata No. 2 in E-flat Major

Johann Sebastian Bach
1685-1750
BWV 1031

Bach wrote few articulations and dynamics, leaving such interpretive details to the performer. The markings here are suggestions. As you study this piece, you may wish to make your own decisions about such matters.

*played:

Siciliano

[mp]

Siciliano

[mf]

Suite in B Minor

Selected Movements

Rondeau

Johann Sebastian Bach
1685-1750
BWV 1067

Bach wrote few articulations and dynamics, leaving such interpretive details to the performer. The markings presented here are suggestions. As you study this piece, you may wish to make your own decisions about such matters.

28

Polonaise

Fine

Fine

Polonaise da Capo

Menuet

Badinerie

Sonata No. 8 in F Major

George Frideric Handel
1685-1759

Handel wrote few articulations and dynamics, leaving such interpretive details to the performer. The markings presented here are suggestions. As you study this piece, you may wish to make your own decisions about such matters.

[attacca]

25

[rit.]

[rit.]

Siciliana (larghetto)

[mp]

Siciliana (larghetto)

[mp]

3

[mf]

[mf]

5

[attacca]

Serenade in C Major

Franz Joseph Haydn
1732-1809

Andante in C Major

Wolfgang Amadeus Mozart
1756-1791
K 315(285e)

Concerto No. 1 in G Major

First Movement

Wolfgang Amadeus Mozart
1756-1791
K 313(285c)

Flute and Piano

THE WORLD'S GREAT CLASSICAL MUSIC

The Baroque and Classical Flute

12 Favorite Pieces by the Masters

EDITED BY ELAINE SCHMIDT
Bryan Stanley, assistant editor

Flute Part

ISBN 978-0-634-02231-9

7777 W. BLUEMOUND RD. P.O. BOX 13819 MILWAUKEE, WI 53213

Visit Hal Leonard Online at
www.halleonard.com

FOREWORD

Playing Baroque music presents both students and professionals with some interesting challenges. Many composers of the Baroque and Classical eras did not write many, if any, dynamic markings or articulation markings in their music. Nor did they indicate all of the trills or other ornaments that were in common use at the time. If an edition of a Bach piece does not include any of these familiar marks, do not assume the composer wanted the music to be played without dynamic contrasts or expressive articulations. Bach, and other composers of his time, left those details up to the performer. The flutist can make a personal statement in part by deciding how to tongue and slur a piece, or how to use dynamic contrasts.

If you are confused about working out interpretive details for a piece of music, you are not alone. There are no absolute rules, but there are lots of opinions. Two hundred-fifty years ago, musical customs differed from one European country to another, and even from one local province to another. Although many composers used the same symbols for ornaments in their music, the symbols did not necessarily mean the same thing to each composer. Since the technology for recording sound was still hundreds of years away, the musicians who played this music when it was new are silent to us. We will never know exactly how they interpreted the music.

There has been an explosion of interest in early music in recent years, sending scholars and musicians off in search of definitive answers on these topics. The research is like musical detective work. There are written sources such as books and teaching materials from the era to be studied. Original music, preserved in libraries, museums, and other collections, can also provide clues. But for a student today, the best way to learn to play Baroque music, or music of any previous era for that matter, is the same way people learned to play it during the years in which it was new—listening. If you want to play Bach, listen to Bach and if you want to play Handel, listen to Handel. Pay close attention to the details and nuances in the performances and try bringing those ideas to your own playing. Listen to other pieces by the same composer, as well as other composers' pieces written at the same time and in the same country or region. This kind of listening helps create a framework for the musical fashion of the era and the interpretive practices in place today. Understanding how the composer's music fits into the time and place in which it was written is also helpful. Besides traditional library research, the Internet is a great place to search for biographies and histories of musicians and the times in which they lived.

This book provides conservative articulation and dynamic suggestions for the various Baroque and Classical pieces, as well as cadenzas for some of them, to give the student a starting point. As you learn the pieces, you and your teacher may choose to alter these marks and make your own decisions. Feel free. This is part of the fun of playing this music.

—Elaine Schmidt

Flute Part
CONTENTS

Sonata in A Minor

(solo flute)

Carl Philipp Emanuel Bach
1714-1788
H. 562

Trills begin on the note above in this historical period.
For instance, see this example:

6

8

Sonata No. 2 in E-flat Major

Johann Sebastian Bach
1685-1750
BWV 1031

12

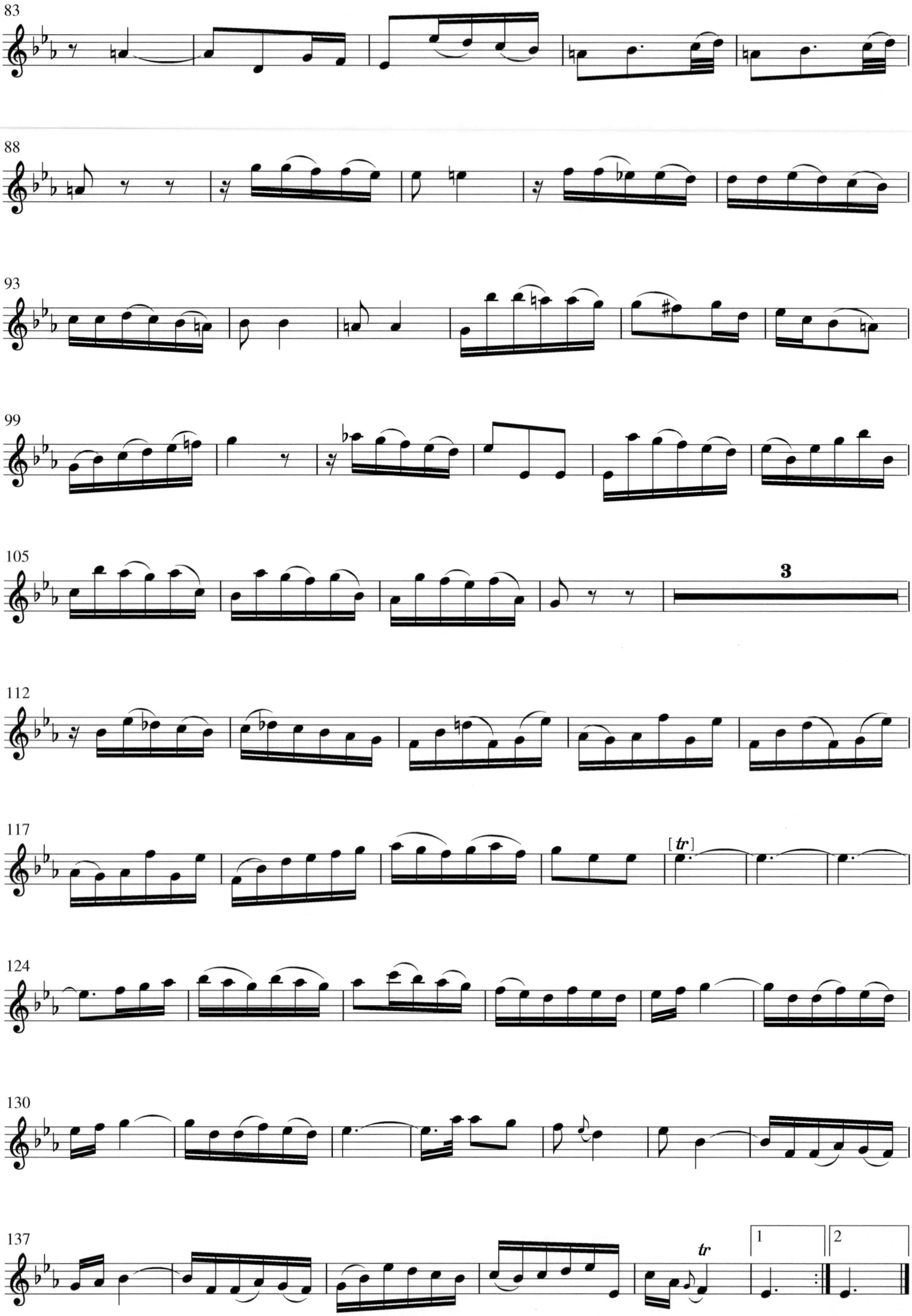
83
88
93
99
105
3
112
117
[tr]
124
130
137
tr
1
2

Sarabande
from the Partita in A Minor (solo flute)

Johann Sebastian Bach
1685-1750
BWV 1013

Bach wrote few articulations and dynamics, leaving such interpretive details to the performer.
The markings presented here are suggestions. As you study this piece, you may wish to make
your own decisions about such matters.

Bourrée Anglaise
from the Partita in A Minor (solo flute)

Johann Sebastian Bach
1685-1750
BWV 1013

Bach wrote few articulations and dynamics, leaving such interpetive details to the performer.
The markings presented here are suggestions. As you study this piece, you may wish to
make your own decisions about such matters.

Suite in B Minor
Selected Movements

Johann Sebastian Bach
1685-1750
BWV 1067

Rondeau

Bach wrote few articulations and dynamics, leaving such interpretive details to the performer. The markings presented here are suggestions. As you study this piece, you may wish to make your own decisions about such matters.

Polonaise

Polonaise da Capo

20

Menuet

Badinerie

Sonata No. 8 in F Major

George Frideric Handel
1685-1759

Handel wrote few articulations and dynamics, leaving such interpretive details to the performer. The markings presented here are suggestions. As you study this piece, you may wish to make your own decisions about such matters.

23

24

Andante in C Major

Wolfgang Amadeus Mozart
1756-1791
K 315(285e)

Serenade in C Major

Franz Joseph Haydn
1732-1809

Andante cantabile

Concerto No. 1 in G Major
First Movement

Wolfgang Amadeus Mozart
1756-1791
K 313(285c)

34

Concerto No. 2 in D Major
Second Movement

Wolfgang Amadeus Mozart
1756-1791
K 314(285d)

Concerto No. 2 in D Major
Third Movement

Wolfgang Amadeus Mozart
1756-1791
K 314

38

Fantasie No. 2 in A Minor
from 12 FANTASIES (solo flute)

Georg Philipp Telemann
1681-1767

Telemann wrote few articulations and dynamics, leaving such interpretive details to the performer. The markings presented here are suggestions. As you study this piece, you may wish to make your own decisions about such matters.

44

Sonata No. 1 in A Minor

Johann Joachim Quantz
1697-1773

Gigue (Allegro)

Suite in A Minor
Selected Movements

Georg Philipp Telemann
1681-1767

Ouverture

Telemann wrote few articulations and dynamics, leaving such interpretive details to the performer. The markings presented here are suggestions. As you study this piece, you may wish to make your own decisions about such matters.

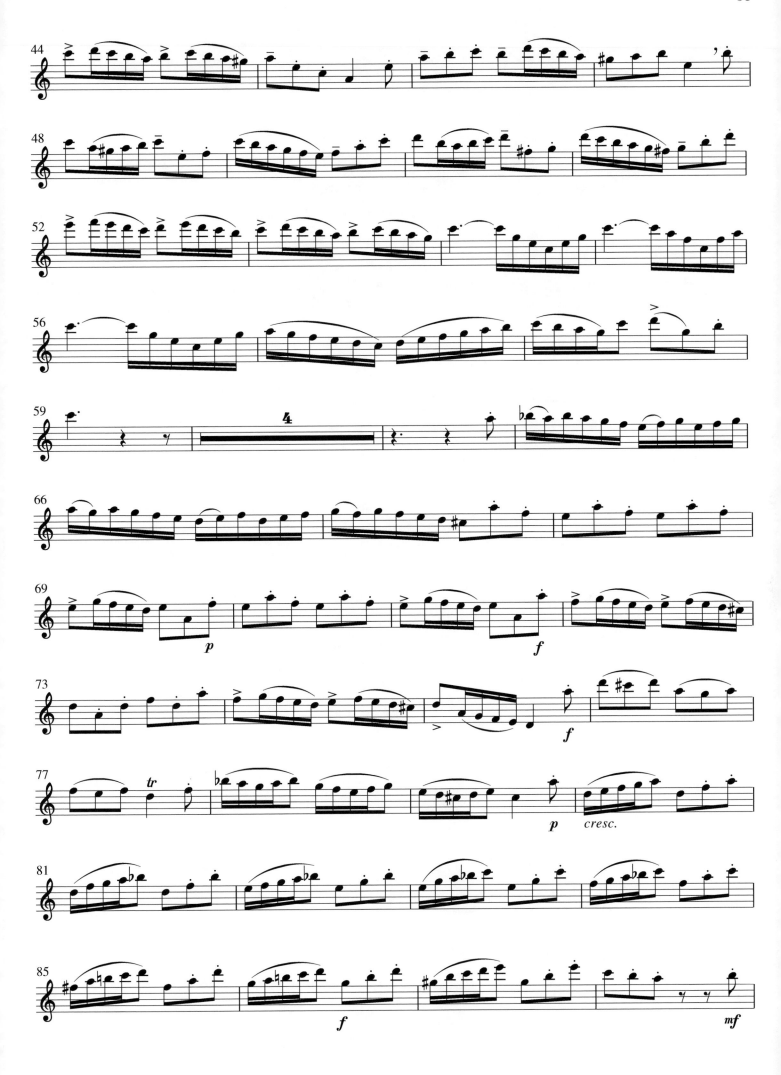

53

Menuet 2

Moderato

[*mf* - *p*]

5

9

[*mp* - *f*]   *p*

13

f

17

[*mp*]   *mf*

21

p   *cresc.*   *f*

25

[*mf*]

29

[*f*]

65

Concerto No. 2 in D Major
Second Movement

Wolfgang Amadeus Mozart
1756-1791
K 314(285d)

Concerto No. 2 in D Major
Third Movement

Wolfgang Amadeus Mozart
1756-1791
K 314

Sonata No. 1 in A Minor

Johann Joachim Quantz
1697-1773

98

Suite in A Minor
Selected Movements

Georg Philipp Telemann
1681-1767

Ouverture

Telemann wrote few articulations and dynamics, leaving such interpretive details to the performer. The markings presented here are suggestions. As you study this piece, you may wish to make your own decisions about such matters.

116

Menuet 2